LES PETITS PLATS
FRANÇAIS
SIMON & SCHUSTER
ILLUSTRATED

cooking en cocotte

JOSÉ MARÉCHAL

Photography by Akiko Ida
Styling by Camille Fourmont

SIMON &
SCHUSTER
ILLUSTRATED

London · New York · Sydney · Toronto
A CBS COMPANY

English language edition published in Great Britain by
Simon and Schuster UK Ltd, 2011
A CBS Company

Copyright © Marabout 2008

SIMON AND SCHUSTER
ILLUSTRATED BOOKS
Simon & Schuster UK
222 Gray's Inn Road
London WC1X 8HB
www.simonandschuster.co.uk

1 2 3 4 5 6 7 8 9 10

Translation: Prudence Ivey
Copy editor English language: Nicki Lampon

Colour reproduction by Dot Gradations Ltd, UK
Printed and bound in U.A.E.

ISBN 978-0-85720-357-1

Contents

Hints and tips for cooking in mini cocottes

Mini cocottes are individual-sized pots or dishes, perfect for creating little sweet and savoury delights.

Preparation
Cut your ingredients into small pieces so they are in scale with the mini cocottes for fast and even cooking. This will also make it easier to eat these mini meals out of the cocottes.

Precooking
Seal pieces of meat, blanch vegetables in boiling water and brown or caramelise some fruits before cooking them in the cocottes in a sauce, stock, broth, wine or cream so that they don't dry out.

Marinating
Condiments, exotic or simple sauces, fruit juices, honey and spices will all add flavour and help to keep your ingredients tender.

Cooking
This is the final step when cooking in mini cocottes. Cook in an oven using one of the following techniques.

In a bain-marie – place the cocottes in a roasting dish with high sides, half filled with water, and cook at a medium heat (180°C/fan oven 160°C/Gas Mark 4).

Braising – cook the ingredients with an aromatic garnish in cocottes that have been half filled with liquid, such as stock, a creamy sauce, marinade, etc.

Roasting – cook your precooked or blanched ingredients in a hot oven (200°C/fan oven 180°C/Gas Mark 6) to give them a pretty golden colour.

portionner ↑

cuire ↓

précuire ↑

mariner ↓

Baked eggs

You can vary this dish in a hundred different ways depending on your mood, the contents of your shopping basket or your Sunday night leftovers.

Use the following simple but delicious recipe and improvise as you like.

Break 2 eggs into the cocotte, add the flavourings of your choice and top up with cream, then cook for 10 minutes in a hot oven (180°C/fan oven 160°C/Gas Mark 4). The white should be just cooked and the yellow still runny. A treat for young and old alike!

Baked eggs enable you to easily create quick recipes adapted to individual tastes and to use the leftovers from your fridge. Light, classic or refined, here are some of my favourite combinations…

Sun-dried tomatoes and pesto
Often served as antipasti or finely chopped in a salad, a few sun-dried tomatoes is enough to beautifully flavour these baked eggs. It's hard not to associate this recipe with basil pesto, which, if added just before serving, turns it into a sunshine-filled dish.

Foie gras
Added to eggs, a slice of this delicacy makes a chic little meal. You don't have to wait till Christmas to treat yourself.

Asparagus and Parma ham
The virtues of asparagus have been known since antiquity – the Greeks dedicated asparagus to the goddess of love… So be bold! Add some precooked asparagus, enhanced with some finely sliced Parma ham, and this dish makes an attention-grabbing, refined meal.

Three cheese and walnut
Nearly all cheeses will work here. Instead of using leftovers in a quiche or omelette, try them in a mini cocotte. The cheese will coat the eggs in a creamy sauce.

Ham and Cheddar
Baked eggs for kids? Yes, but grown ups will love this too!

Fresh herbs
A lighter dish (sort of). Finely chopped chives, parsley, coriander, tarragon or mint will flavour these eggs quickly and easily.

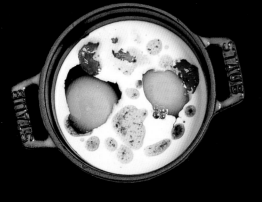

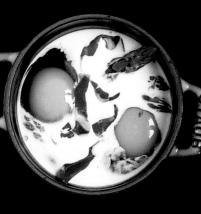
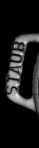

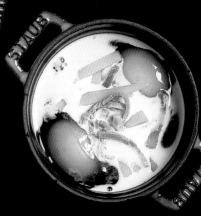

Baked eggs in red wine sauce

Preparation time: 30 minutes
Cooking time: 7–8 minutes
Serves 6–8

750 ml (26 fl oz) red wine
1 teaspoon caster sugar
50 g (1¾ oz) butter
3 shallots, finely chopped
1 onion, finely chopped
180 g (6¼ oz) smoked lardons
6–8 eggs
freshly ground black pepper
wholemeal bread, to serve

Pour the wine into a saucepan and bring to the boil. As soon as it starts boiling, remove the pan from the heat and flambé the wine to burn off the alcohol.

Return the pan to a low heat, add the sugar and leave the wine to reduce by half until it reaches a syrupy consistency.

Meanwhile, melt the butter in a pan and cook the shallots and onion over a low heat for around 15 minutes until they are very soft. Add the lardons and cook for around 5 minutes. Drain off the fat through a sieve and set aside.

Preheat the oven to 180°C (fan oven 160°C), Gas Mark 4.

Divide the lardon mixture between the cocottes and pour over the wine sauce until they are half filled.

Half fill a roasting tin with hot water and place the cocottes in it. Carefully break an egg into the centre of each.

Cook for around 7–8 minutes. Finish with some black pepper and serve immediately with wholemeal toasted soldiers.

Basque eggs

Preparation time: 45 minutes
Cooking time: 7–8 minutes
Serves 6–8

3 tablespoons olive oil
2 garlic cloves, crushed
2 onions, finely chopped
2 red peppers, de-seeded and
  finely chopped
2 yellow peppers, de-seeded
  and finely chopped
2 pinches of ground Espelette
  pepper
2 pinches of caster sugar
230 g canned tomatoes
salt and freshly ground black pepper
6–8 eggs

Heat the oil in a saucepan and cook the garlic over a medium heat. Add the onions and peppers and leave to sweat then add the Espelette pepper, sugar and tomatoes. Season and cook over a low heat for 20–25 minutes, stirring occasionally.

Preheat the oven to 180°C (fan oven 160°C), Gas Mark 4.

Divide the sauce between the cocottes.

Half fill a roasting tin with hot water and place the cocottes in it. Carefully break an egg in the centre of each dish and cook for 7–8 minutes.

Tip: Espelette peppers are a type of mild chilli grown in the Basque region. Ground Espelette pepper is available from specialist food shops or online, but if you can't find it you could use paprika instead.

Poached eggs with goats' cheese and mint

Preparation time: 30 minutes
Cooking time: 4–5 minutes
Serves 6–8

125 ml (4½ fl oz) white vinegar
12–16 eggs, at room temperature
1 litre (1¾ pints) single cream
2 tablespoons mascarpone
salt and freshly ground black pepper
a bunch of fresh mint, finely
  chopped
6–8 rounds of goats' cheese,
  around 1 cm (½ inch) thick

Fill a saucepan with water, add the vinegar and heat until it begins to bubble slightly.

Meanwhile, break an egg into a ramekin. Gently slide the eggs, one by one, into the simmering water, leave to poach for 3 minutes then remove from the water with a slotted spoon and place in cold water to cool for 1–2 minutes. Drain the eggs and place on kitchen towel.

In a different saucepan, gently heat the cream and mascarpone. Season and leave to reduce over a low heat for around 8 minutes.

Preheat the grill to high to brown the cheese to perfection or preheat the oven to 220°C (fan oven 200°C), Gas Mark 7.

Add 2 eggs to each cocotte, cover with the mascarpone cream, sprinkle with the mint and top with a round of goats' cheese.

Cook for around 4–5 minutes, keeping a close eye on the eggs to ensure they do not burn. The eggs are already poached and so should not cook any further. The cheese should melt in the cream and brown lightly.

Tip: The poached eggs can be prepared in advance and kept in a bowl of water covered with cling film in the fridge.

Vegetable cocottes

These suggestions for vegetable pots are directly inspired by the traditional Provençale tian, in which aubergines, courgettes and tomatoes are usually used. They make a great light meal on their own, or a tasty and original accompaniment for your favourite dishes. Use seasonal ingredients and beautiful colours.

The autumnal
This mini cocotte of artichokes, chestnuts and potatoes goes perfectly with a roast chicken or game bird. For winter, spring and summer, improvise with other seasonal ingredients.

The blue
Finely chop courgette and celery, lightly blanch in boiling water and alternate with slices of Roquefort or another blue cheese before cooking for around 15 minutes in a hot oven.

The 'très Français'
I never tire of my mother's chicory in ham. Nowadays this dish isn't quite as popular as it deserves to be, or maybe it has aged badly. A little reworking is essential. Replace the chicory with some lightly blanched leeks, wrap in sliced ham and add a few slices of Gruyère cheese to melt goldenly over the whole.

The Provençale
Aubergines, courgettes, tomatoes and mozzarella; all the flavours of my childhood in a mini cocotte with the taste of the South of France.

The Italian
Aubergines, pieces of parmesan and grilled pine nuts prettily arranged in a cocotte and baked will make a great meal all on its own.

The very very green
There is an incredible variety of green vegetables. Some of them aren't always popular with kids or even adults. Blanched, with some butter stirred in, and then cooked in a mini cocotte with some ricotta for around 15 minutes, and this healthy selection of green vegetables will be popular with everyone.

Braised mixed vegetables

Preparation time: 30 minutes
Cooking time: 30 minutes
Serves 6–8

200 g (7 oz) carrots, peeled and
  cut into large chunks
150 g (5¼ oz) parsnips, peeled
  and cut into large chunks
150 g (5¼ oz) Jerusalem artichokes,
  peeled and cut into large chunks
125 g (4½ oz) mange tout, topped
  and tailed
5 artichoke hearts, quartered
8 baby spring onions, trimmed
2 tablespoons olive oil
500 ml (18 fl oz) vegetable stock
4 shallots, finely chopped
125 g (4½ oz) salted butter, at
  room temperature
salt and freshly ground black pepper
½ a bunch of fresh flat leaf parsley,
  finely chopped
½ a bunch of fresh coriander,
  finely chopped
½ a bunch of fresh basil, finely
  chopped

Preheat the oven to 170°C (fan oven
150°C), Gas Mark 3½.

Using a heavy-based saucepan,
lightly brown the carrots, parsnips,
Jerusalem artichokes, mange tout,
artichoke hearts and spring onions
in the olive oil for 2–3 minutes.

Divide the vegetables evenly
between the cocottes then add the
stock. Cover and leave to simmer
in the oven for around 30 minutes,
checking them occasionally and
adding a little more liquid if
necessary.

Meanwhile, mix the shallots with
the butter and season. Keep at room
temperature.

Check that the vegetables are
cooked using the point of a knife.

Add a knob of shallot butter to each
cocotte, sprinkle with the herbs and
serve immediately.

Curried carrots with gingerbread

Preparation time: 30 minutes
Cooking time: 35–40 minutes
Serves 6–8

800 g (1 lb 11 oz) carrots, peeled
4 egg yolks
250 ml (9 fl oz) milk
250 ml (9 fl oz) single cream
1 scant teaspoon curry powder
salt and freshly ground black pepper
12–16 gingerbread slices

Using a grater or mandolin, cut the carrots into very thin slices. Bring a pan of water to the boil, add the carrots and blanch for 1–2 minutes to soften them. Remove with a slotted spoon and plunge into cold water.

Mix the egg yolks, milk, cream and curry powder together and season.

Trim the gingerbread slices until they fit the shape of the cocottes.

Preheat the oven to 170°C (fan oven 150°C), Gas Mark 3½.

Half fill a roasting tin with hot water and place the cocottes in it.

Place a round of gingerbread in the bottom of each cocotte and cover with slices of carrot, pressing down well. Pour over the cream mixture to cover and top with another slice of gingerbread before finishing with the remaining cream mixture.

Cook in the oven for 35–40 minutes.

Tip: These cocottes taste equally good hot or cold.

Mini potato gratin with mushrooms and spinach

Preparation time: 25 minutes
Cooking time: 35 minutes
Serves 6–8

800 g (1 lb 12 oz) potatoes,
  peeled and sliced
150 g (5¼ oz) mushrooms,
  finely sliced
600 g (1 lb 5 oz) crème fraîche
2 garlic cloves, crushed
a couple of pinches of grated
  nutmeg
200 g (7 oz) fresh spinach,
  washed and chopped
salt and freshly ground black pepper

Layer the potato and mushroom slices in the cocottes, alternating the layers until the cocottes are half filled.

Preheat the oven to 180°C (fan oven 160°C), Gas Mark 4.

Mix the crème fraîche, garlic, nutmeg and spinach together. Season. Divide this mixture between the cocottes and cook for around 35 minutes.

Mini cheese fondue with vegetables

Preparation time: 30 minutes
Cooking time: 10–12 minutes
Serves 6–8

125 g (8 oz) Comté cheese
125 g (8 oz) Gruyère cheese
125 g (8 oz) Cheddar cheese
1 litre (1¾ pints) white wine
1 garlic clove, crushed
3 generous gratings of black pepper
1 kg (2 lb 4 oz) raw or cooked
  vegetables of your choice (carrots,
  radishes, mushrooms, celery,
  etc.), peeled if necessary and
  chopped into bite-sized pieces

Grate the cheeses, or cut into small cubes, and set aside in the fridge.

Gently heat the white wine with the crushed garlic and the pepper. Leave to simmer and, little by little, reduce the wine by half.

Preheat the oven to 170°C (fan oven 150°C), Gas Mark 3½.

Divide the reduced wine and cheeses between the cocottes. Cover and cook in the oven for around 10–12 minutes until the cheese is completely melted.

Serve the cocottes straight from the oven with the assorted vegetables for dipping into the fondue.

Tip: Comté cheese is a cow's milk cheese made in the Franche-Comté region of France. If you can't find it easily, try using extra Gruyère or Emmental cheese.

Pea, ham and Boursin clafoutis

Preparation time: 15 minutes
Cooking time: 20–25 minutes
Serves 4–5

70 g (2½ oz) Boursin
1 egg yolk
4 eggs
60 g (2 oz) cornflour
150 ml (5¼ fl oz) single cream
200 ml (7 fl oz) milk
salt and freshly ground black pepper
3–4 slices of ham, cut into
  small pieces
200 g (7 oz) peas (fresh or frozen)

Gently whisk the Boursin and egg yolk together. Still whisking, add the whole eggs one by one followed by the cornflour. Add the cream and milk little by little, whisk until well combined then season and set aside in the fridge.

Preheat the oven to 180°C (fan oven 160°C), Gas Mark 4.

Mix the ham with the peas and divide between the cocottes. Half fill a roasting tin with hot water and place the cocottes in it.

Add the Boursin mixture to the cocottes and cook, uncovered, for 20–25 minutes.

Potato and bacon gratin

Preparation time: 35 minutes
Cooking time: 30 minutes
Serves 4–6

200 ml (7 fl oz) white wine
1 onion, finely chopped
200 ml (7 fl oz) double cream
1 garlic clove, halved
1 kg (2 lb 4 oz) potatoes, peeled
   and thinly sliced
salt and freshly ground black pepper
a couple of pinches of grated
   nutmeg
1 reblochon cheese, thinly sliced
100 g (3½ oz) lardons

Pour the wine into a saucepan, add the onion and heat for 3–4 minutes. Add the cream and leave to reduce for a further 2–3 minutes. Set aside away from the heat.

Preheat the oven to 180°C (fan oven 160°C), Gas Mark 4.

Rub the garlic clove around the inside of the cocottes.

Put a layer of potato at the bottom of the cocottes, sprinkle with a little salt (be sparing as this dish can be quite salty), pepper and nutmeg then add a layer of cheese and a few lardons. Repeat until the cocotte is two-thirds full. Finish with a slice of cheese and then pour over the cream mixture.

Cook for 30 minutes, covering halfway through (once the tops are nice and golden) to make sure the cocottes do not dry out.

Tip: Reblochon is a creamy cheese from the Alps region of France. It is available from some supermarkets, specialist delis or online. If you can't find it, try using a good Brie or Camembert.

Potato soufflé

Preparation time: 50 minutes +
cooling
Cooking time: 15 minutes
Serves 6–8

500 g (1 lb 2 oz) potatoes, peeled
120 g (4¼ oz) softened butter
12 thin slices smoked streaky
bacon
a couple of pinches of grated
nutmeg
salt and freshly ground black pepper
4 egg whites, at room temperature

Fill a large saucepan with cold salted
water, bring to the boil and cook the
potatoes for 25–30 minutes
(depending on their size).

While the potatoes are cooking,
brush the inside of the cocottes with
two-thirds of the butter and put in the
fridge for 8–10 minutes.

Finely chop the bacon (setting aside
2–3 whole slices for garnish).

Drain the potatoes, allow to cool and
mash, adding the remaining butter.
Add the nutmeg and the pieces of
bacon and season to taste.

Preheat the oven to 210°C (fan oven
190°C), Gas Mark 6½.

Whisk the egg whites with a pinch
of salt and gently fold them into the
mashed potato.

Fill the cocottes to just below the
edge and smooth with a spatula.

Cook for 15 minutes: the mix should
rise and become lightly golden. Grill
the remaining pieces of bacon and
use to garnish the cocottes. Serve
immediately.

Cheese and herb ravioli in chicken stock

Preparation time: 10 minutes
Cooking time: 5 minutes
Serves 6–8

750 ml (26 fl oz) chicken stock
300 g (10½ oz) mini ravioli (ravioles
  de Royan)
a bunch of fresh coriander
freshly ground black pepper

Preheat the oven to 170°C (fan oven 150°C), Gas Mark 3½.

Bring the chicken stock to the boil then pour the hot stock into the cocottes until they are two-thirds full. Add the ravioli.

Sprinkle with coriander leaves, season with pepper then cover and cook for around 5 minutes.

Tip: Ravioles de Royan are mini ravioli stuffed with cheese and herbs. Look for them in specialist delis or online.

Lentil and smoked sausage stew

Preparation time: 40 minutes
Cooking time: 25 minutes
Serves 6–8

80 g (2¾ oz) green lentils
80 g (2¾ oz) black lentils
80 g (2¾ oz) red lentils
salt
750 ml (26 fl oz) chicken stock
1 onion, chopped
1 sprig of thyme
1 bay leaf
½ smoked sausage
2 dessertspoons wholegrain
   mustard

Place the three types of lentil in three separate pans of cold salted water and leave to cook over a medium heat. The red lentils will take 10 minutes; the green and black lentils will take 20 minutes.

Bring the chicken stock to the boil with the onion, thyme, bay leaf and sausage and cook on a rolling boil for around 10 minutes.

Drain the lentils and rinse in cold water.

Preheat the oven to 200°C (fan oven 180°C), Gas Mark 6.

Strain the stock and mix in the mustard. Peel the sausage and cut into semi-circular slices.

Share the lentils between the cocottes, pour over the stock until half filled and add the slices of sausage. Cover and cook for 25 minutes.

Tip: Black lentils are usually available in health food or ethnic stores.

Pork ribs with caramelised baby new potatoes

Preparation time: 1 hour
Cooking time: 30 minutes
Makes 6–8

800 g–1 kg (1 lb 12 oz–2 lb 4 oz)
   pork ribs
2 tablespoons sunflower oil
40 g (1½ oz) butter
20 g (¾ oz) caster sugar
400 g (14 oz) baby new potatoes,
   peeled
2 onions, sliced
100 ml (3½ fl oz) white wine
salt and freshly ground black pepper
400 ml (14 fl oz) hoisin sauce (or
   use the marinade on page 38)

Cut the ribs into small portions, making sure that there are at least two bones per portion. Clean the bones with a small knife so that they look a bit more attractive (or you can ask your butcher to do this for you).

Put the ribs in a saucepan half filled with cold salted water and bring to the boil. Cook on a medium heat for 20 minutes.

Heat the oil, butter and sugar in a pan with high sides. Add the potatoes and onions and cook until gently caramelised. Add the wine, season and leave to cook over a low heat until the liquid has evaporated.

Preheat the oven to 180°C (fan oven 160°C), Gas Mark 4.

Drain and rinse the ribs. Brush with the hoisin sauce or marinade then divide between the cocottes with the potatoes and onions.

Add 2 tablespoons of water to each cocotte and cook for around 30 minutes.

Chicken with potatoes and fruit

Preparation time: 1 hour
Cooking time: 30 minutes
Serves 6–8

3 x 600 g (1 lb 5 oz) poussins
200 g (7 oz) blue or purple
   potatoes (e.g. Vitelotte)
50 ml (2 fl oz) sunflower oil
50 g (1¾ oz) butter
3–4 dessert apples (e.g. Jonagold),
   peeled, cored and quartered
salt and freshly ground black pepper
150 ml (5 fl oz) raspberry vinegar
125 g (4½ oz) raspberries
500 ml (18 fl oz) cider

Cut the poussins in half lengthways then separate the legs and thighs.

With pliers, remove the wings and tips of the legs for a more attractive appearance.

Put the potatoes in a saucepan and cover with cold water. Salt generously (so that they keep their colour), bring to the boil and cook for 15 minutes. Drain.

Heat the oil and butter and seal the poussin pieces and apples to precook them and give them colour. Season and add the vinegar. Set aside away from the heat.

Preheat the oven to 200°C (fan oven 180°C), Gas Mark 6.

Fill the cocottes with the poussin pieces, apples, potatoes and raspberries and add a splash of cider to each. Cook for 30 minutes.

Thai chicken and prawns

Preparation time: 30 minutes +
overnight marinating
Cooking time: 25–30 minutes
Serves 6–8

3 garlic cloves, finely chopped
40 g (1½ oz) fresh root ginger,
  finely chopped
80 ml (3 fl oz) tomato ketchup
1 tablespoon honey
50 ml (2 fl oz) soy sauce
200 ml (7 fl oz) beef stock
6–8 chicken drumsticks
12–16 large raw prawns, shelled
  but with tails left on
12–16 baby corn (fresh or frozen)
  (optional)
80 g (2¾ oz) sesame seeds
½ bunch of fresh coriander, to serve

The day before, mix the garlic and
ginger with the ketchup, honey, soy
sauce and beef stock. Place the
chicken drumsticks and prawns in a
large bowl, mix with the marinade
and leave to marinate in the fridge
overnight.

The next day, preheat the oven
to 170°C (fan oven 150°C), Gas
Mark 3½.

Fill each cocotte with a drumstick,
2 prawns and 2 baby corn, if using.

Mix any leftover marinade with
a little water and pour into the
cocottes. Sprinkle with the sesame
seeds and cook for 25–30 minutes.

Add a few leaves of coriander then
serve immediately.

Duck with lemon and sage

Preparation time: 1 hour
Cooking time: 15 minutes
Serves 6–8

4 lemons, cut into sixths
200 g (7 oz) caster sugar
5–6 duck legs
100 g (3½ oz) breadcrumbs
30 g (1 oz) butter, at room
  temperature
2 garlic cloves, finely chopped
a small bunch of fresh sage, a few
  leaves reserved for decoration and
  the remainder finely chopped

Place the lemons, sugar and 1 litre (1¾ pints) of water in a saucepan over a medium heat and leave to cook until the liquid has almost entirely evaporated (about 40 minutes). Set aside at room temperature. (To save time you could do this in advance.)

Preheat the oven to 180°C (fan oven 160°C), Gas Mark 4. Place the duck legs in a roasting tray and cook for about 15 minutes to remove as much fat as possible.

Mix the breadcrumbs, butter, garlic and a few chopped sage leaves together and knead with your fingertips.

Remove the bones from the duck legs, taking care to keep the flesh in large pieces, and share the meat between the cocottes. Cut a few of the lemons into smaller pieces and add to the cocottes with the bigger slices. Sprinkle with the breadcrumb mixture and cook for around 15 minutes.

Remove from the oven, add a few sage leaves for decoration and serve immediately.

Prawn and asparagus with Parmesan cheese

Preparation time: 45 minutes
Cooking time: 8 minutes
Serves 6–8

2 bunches of asparagus
16 large raw prawns
400 ml (14 fl oz) single cream
400 g (14 oz) Parmesan cheese
salt and freshly ground black pepper
200 g (7 oz) breadcrumbs

Bring a pan of water to the boil, add the asparagus and cook for 10 minutes. It should remain firm.

Meanwhile, remove the shells from the prawns, leaving the heads and tails attached. Shave the Parmesan with a vegetable peeler.

Carefully remove the asparagus from the water, cool and spread on kitchen towel to dry. Cut each spear in half and set aside the tips.

Blend the bottoms of the asparagus spears with the cream and a little Parmesan. Season lightly.

Preheat the oven to 180°C (fan oven 160°C), Gas Mark 4.

Divide the asparagus cream between the cocottes.

Roll the prawns and asparagus spears in the breadcrumbs then add them, heads and tips in the air, to the cocottes. Scatter the remaining Parmesan over the top and cook for 8 minutes.

Shellfish in cider

Preparation time: 25 minutes
Cooking time: 6 minutes
Serves 6–8

750 ml (26 fl oz) cider
400 g (14 oz) mussels, cleaned
200 g (7 oz) cockles, cleaned
200 g (7 oz) clams, cleaned
freshly ground black pepper
3–4 shallots, finely chopped
½ bunch fresh parsley or chervil
200 g (7 oz) crème fraîche (optional)
12 baby carrots, peeled and cooked
  (optional)

Heat the cider in a saucepan and leave to boil for 2 minutes.

Add the shellfish to the hot cider, season with pepper and stir until the shells open slightly. Discard any that remain closed.

Preheat the oven to 170°C (fan oven 150°C), Gas Mark 3½.

Divide the shallots and shellfish between the cocottes. Filter the cider through a very fine sieve or muslin cloth to remove any sand, then pour over the shellfish.

Loosely cover the cocottes with aluminium foil and cook for around 6 minutes.

Sprinkle with the parsley or chervil and top with a small spoonful of crème fraîche and small cooked carrots, if using. Serve immediately.

Tip: If you wish, add the crème fraîche before putting the cocottes in the oven so that it melts and mixes with the cider.

Mini bouillabaisse

Preparation time: 45 minutes
Cooking time: 25 minutes
Serves 6–8

400 g (14 oz) potatoes, peeled
  and cut into thick rounds
a couple of pinches of saffron
50 ml (2 fl oz) pastis
6–8 crayfish
1 litre (1¾ pints) fish stock
6–8 red mullet fillets
300 g (10½ oz) scorpion fish,
  conger eel or John Dory fillets
300 g (10½ oz) mussels, cleaned
salt and freshly ground black pepper

Add the potatoes, half the saffron
and the pastis to a saucepan filled
with cold salted water. Bring to the
boil and cook for 8 minutes. The
potatoes should remain firm. Gently
remove the potatoes from the water
and set both aside.

Meanwhile, remove the crayfish
shells, setting aside the head and
the tail, and cut the flesh into small
pieces.

Preheat the oven to 170°C (fan oven
150°C), Gas Mark 3½.

Mix the remaining saffron and the
fish stock with the potato cooking
water, then heat until just simmering.
Pour into the cocottes.

Add 1–2 slices of potato to the
bottom of each cocotte and top with
the crayfish, fish fillets and mussels.
Finish with the remaining potatoes.

Cook for around 25 minutes.

Tip: A bouillabaisse is traditionally
served in two stages, the stock with
croûtons and a rouille, followed by the
fish and potatoes. You could serve
this mini bouillabaisse with a few
croûtons spread with rouille to dunk
in the soup.

Scallops in a tea and lemongrass broth

Preparation time: 1 hour
Cooking time: 6–7 minutes
Serves 6–8

1 Chinese cabbage
1 litre (1¾ pints) vegetable stock
20 g (¾ oz) caster sugar
2 lemongrass stems, finely chopped
25 g (1 oz) tea leaves
2 tablespoons olive oil
6–8 scallops
salt and freshly ground black pepper

Remove the centre of the cabbage and chop the leaves finely.

Fill a saucepan with salted water and bring to the boil. Blanch the cabbage for 2 minutes then drain and cool in cold running water. Set aside.

Place the vegetable stock, sugar and lemongrass in a pan and bring to the boil. Remove from the heat, add the tea and leave to infuse.

Meanwhile, heat the oil over a high heat and sear the scallops for 1 minute on each side. Remove from the pan and place on a sheet of kitchen towel.

Preheat the oven to 180°C (fan oven 160°C), Gas Mark 4.

Half fill the cocottes with the blanched cabbage.

Strain the infused vegetable stock to remove the lemongrass and tea leaves then pour into the cocottes so that the cabbage is well covered.

Add a scallop to each cocotte, season then cover and cook in the oven for 6–7 minutes. Serve immediately.

Scallops and snails with croûtons

Preparation time: 25 minutes
Cooking time: 8–10 minutes
Serves 6–8

4 garlic cloves, finely chopped
a bunch of fresh flat leaf parsley,
  finely chopped
150 g (5¼ oz) salted butter,
  softened
8 slices white bread, cut into
  small cubes
80 g (2¾ oz) flaked almonds
salt and freshly ground black pepper
48 tinned snails
300 g (10½ oz) small scallops,
  corals removed
400 ml (14 fl oz) white wine

Mix the garlic and parsley with the butter. Set aside at room temperature.

Mix the bread with the almonds and brown in a pan for 2–3 minutes with a little of the garlic and parsley butter. Season.

Preheat the oven to 200°C (fan oven 180°C), Gas Mark 6.

Divide the snails and scallops between the cocottes, season, pour over a dash of white wine and add a knob of parsley butter to each.

Cover with the croûtons and almonds and cook for 8–10 minutes.

Cod and chorizo in a red pepper sauce

Preparation time: 1 hour
Cooking time: 20 minutes
Serves 6–8

4 red peppers
100 ml (3½ fl oz) olive oil
500 g (1 lb 2 oz) cod fillets
 with the skin on
1 onion, chopped
2 garlic cloves, chopped
1 teaspoon tomato purée
salt and freshly ground black pepper
8 chorizo slices

Preheat the oven to 220°C (fan oven 200°C), Gas Mark 7.

Place the peppers on a baking tray and drizzle over some of the olive oil. Cook for 20–25 minutes. The skins of the peppers should be almost burnt. Cover with aluminium foil and leave to cool at room temperature.

Meanwhile, cut the cod into large chunks of around 70 g (2½ oz) each and set aside.

Cut the peppers in half, remove the core and seeds and peel.

In a pan, heat the remaining oil, soften the onion and garlic (without browning) for 3–4 minutes, then add the peppers, tomato purée and 100 ml (3½ fl oz) of water. Season, mix well and leave to cook for 5 minutes.

Remove the peppers from the heat and blend to a coulis (if the mixture is too thick you can add a little water).

Half fill the cocottes with the sauce then add a piece of cod and a slice of chorizo to each. Season lightly, cover and cook in the oven for 20 minutes.

Tip: You could replace the water in the pepper sauce with single cream to make a richer creamy sauce.

Fillet of sole with spinach, topped with meringue and almonds

Preparation time: 40 minutes +
overnight defrosting
Cooking time: 25 minutes
Serves 6–8

1 kg (2 lb 4 oz) frozen spinach
18–24 small sole fillets (you will
need 3 per cocotte)
salt and freshly ground black pepper
spicy sauce (chilli or Asian)
4 egg whites
50 g (1¾ oz) caster sugar
120 g (4¼ oz) flaked almonds

Put the spinach in a sieve and leave
to defrost overnight.

The next day, squash the spinach to
remove all the excess water and then
make small cylindrical balls (similar in
size to the sole fillets).

Place the sole fillets flat on the work
surface, season and drizzle with a
little spicy sauce. Place a spinach ball
at one end of each fillet then roll the
fish around the spinach.

Preheat the oven to 150°C (fan oven
130°C), Gas Mark 2.

Whisk the egg whites until firm,
add the sugar and continue beating
vigorously until they form stiff peaks.

Divide the sole fillets between the
cocottes, season and add a little spicy
sauce to each. Using a spatula, cover
the cocottes with the meringue
mixture.

Sprinkle with the almonds and cook
for 25 minutes.

Tip: You could make these cocottes
a day in advance and keep them in
the fridge, covered with cling film.
On the day you will just have to
make the meringue and cook them.

Watercress and salmon pot pies

Preparation time: 1 hour +
15 minutes chilling
Cooking time: 15 minutes
Serves 8

20 g (¾ oz) butter
1 garlic clove, finely chopped
½ celery stick, finely chopped
½ leek, finely chopped
salt and freshly ground black pepper
600 g (1 lb 5 oz) salmon fillets,
    skin removed
150 ml (5 fl oz) single cream
2 good bunches watercress,
    washed
a pinch of grated nutmeg
1 sheet ready rolled puff pastry
3 egg yolks
poppy or sesame seeds for
    garnish (optional)

Melt the butter in a saucepan over a medium heat. Add the garlic, celery and leek and sweat for 1–2 minutes. Add 1.5 litres (2¾ pints) of water, season generously with salt and bring to the boil.

Meanwhile, cut the salmon into cubes of around 40 g (1½ oz) and set aside in the fridge.

Add the cream to the vegetable water, leave to reduce gently for around 10 minutes then add the watercress. Cook for a further 5–7 minutes.

Remove the watercress mixture from the heat, blend, add the nutmeg and check the seasoning. Leave to cool a little then half fill the cocottes and add the salmon pieces.

Unroll the pastry and cut out eight 13 cm (5 inch) rounds. Brush around the outside edges of the pastry circles with water. Cover the cocottes with the pastry, wet side down, and press the edges down so they stick to the sides of the pots. Beat the egg yolks with a little more water and a pinch of salt and brush over the tops of the pastry.

Preheat the oven to 200°C (fan oven 180°C), Gas Mark 6.

Put the cocottes in the fridge for 15 minutes then cook for another 15 minutes.

Tips: You can make these cocottes the day before and keep them in the fridge before baking.

Brioche with Camembert and redcurrant jelly

Preparation time: 20 minutes
Cooking time: 15 minutes
Serves 6–8

18–20 brioche slices
2 Camembert, thinly sliced
freshly ground black pepper
500 ml (18 fl oz) single cream
1 jar redcurrant jelly, to serve

Trim the brioche slices so that they are roughly the same shape and size as the cocottes.

Preheat the oven to 200°C (fan oven 180°C), Gas Mark 6.

Place a slice of brioche in the bottom of each cocotte, add some Camembert and a little pepper. Continue until the cocottes are half filled. Press down firmly and finish with 1 or 2 slices of Camembert. Cover with the cream and cook for 15 minutes.

Serve warm with the redcurrant jelly.

Totally chocolate

Preparation time: 20 minutes + at least 30 minutes chilling
Cooking time: 7–8 minutes
Serves 4–6

200 g (7 oz) dark chocolate, broken into small pieces
125 g (4½ oz) butter, cubed, plus 50 g (1¾ oz) for greasing, softened
60 g (2 oz) plain flour
20 g (¾ oz) potato flour
20 g (¾ oz) cocoa powder
125 g (4½ oz) caster sugar
3 eggs

Melt the chocolate and butter in a bowl placed over a pan of simmering water.

Mix the two flours and cocoa powder together.

Add the sugar to the melted chocolate then add the eggs and whisk vigorously together.

Add the flour mixture to the chocolate and mix together until you have a smooth paste.

Grease the insides of the cocottes with the softened butter.

Divide the chocolate mixture between the cocottes and put in the fridge for at least 30 minutes (overnight would be even better).

Preheat the oven to 200°C (fan oven 180°C), Gas Mark 6.

Cook for 7–8 minutes. Serve immediately.

Tip: Potato flour is available from health food shops.

Fruit in dessert wine with spiced custard

Preparation time: 30 minutes
Cooking time: 2–3 minutes
Serves 6–8

400–500 g (14 oz–1 lb 2 oz)
mixed seasonal fruits, peeled if
necessary and cut into equal
sized pieces
400 ml (14 fl oz) dessert wine
(e.g. Sauternes)
8 egg yolks
250 g (8¾ oz) caster sugar
10 g (¼ oz) mixed spices (e.g.
vanilla, ground cinnamon, ground
ginger, ground cardamom)

Share the fruit equally among the cocottes and leave to marinate in a little of the wine.

Preheat the grill or heat the oven to 180°C (fan oven 160°C), Gas Mark 4.

In a bowl over a pan of simmering water, whisk the egg yolks vigorously with the sugar and spices until the mixture pales, thickens and doubles in volume (this should take around 15 minutes). Remove from the heat and add the rest of the wine.

Cover the fruits with the spiced custard then put in the oven or leave to brown under the grill for around 2–3 minutes.

Brioche with coconut milk, raspberries and pistachios

Preparation time: 25 minutes
Cooking time: 20–25 minutes
Serves 6–8

18–20 brioche slices
6 egg yolks
120 g (4¼ oz) caster sugar
50 ml (2 fl oz) rum
200 ml (7 fl oz) single cream
400 ml (14 fl oz) coconut milk
125 g (4½ oz) raspberries
50 g (1¾ oz) shelled pistachio nuts

Trim the brioche slices so that they are roughly the same shape and size as the cocottes.

Whisk the egg yolks, sugar and rum together then add the cream and coconut milk. Beat well and set aside.

Preheat the oven to 170°C (fan oven 150°C), Gas Mark 3½. Half fill a roasting tin with hot water ready to go in the oven.

Place the slices of brioche in the cream mixture so they are soaked.

Place a slice of brioche in the bottom of each cocotte, sprinkle with a few raspberries and pistachios and repeat until the cocottes are half filled. Share the rest of the cream between the cocottes then put in the roasting tin.

Cook for 20–25 minutes.

Tip: These can be eaten hot or warm, served with thick cream, or even cold, served with a layer of raspberry coulis.

Apple soufflés

Preparation time: 40 minutes +
10 minutes chilling
Cooking time: 12–15 minutes
Serves 6–8

4–5 dessert apples (e.g. Jonagold),
peeled, cored and cut into chunks
40 g (1½ oz) caster sugar
50 g (1¾ oz) butter, softened
5 egg whites
a pinch of salt

Place the apples in a saucepan over a medium heat with half the sugar and a small glass of water. Cook until the liquid has evaporated and you have a thick compote. Set aside.

Preheat the oven to 210°C (fan oven 190°C), Gas Mark 6½.

Grease the cocottes with the butter then put in the fridge for around 10 minutes.

Whisk the egg whites with the salt until they form stiff peaks, adding the remaining sugar halfway through.

Gently fold the egg whites into the compote.

Fill the cocottes with the apple mixture, smooth with a spatula and wipe the edges of the cocottes so that the mixture rises during cooking (like a soufflé).

Cook for 12–15 minutes and serve immediately.

Apple and prune pies

Preparation time: 40 minutes +
at least 30 minutes soaking
Cooking time: 6–7 minutes
Serves 6–8

150 g (5¼ oz) caster sugar
300 ml (10 fl oz) Calvados
  or Armagnac
30 prunes, stoned
6–8 dessert apples, peeled,
  cored and quartered
120 g (4¼ oz) butter
20 g (¾ oz) soft brown sugar
6–8 filo pastry sheets

In a saucepan, dissolve half the caster sugar with a small glass of water and half the alcohol then heat gently until just bubbling.

Pour the warm syrup on to the prunes and leave to soak for at least 30 minutes.

Meanwhile, place the apples in a saucepan with the remaining caster sugar, alcohol and a large knob of butter. Cook over a medium heat for 7–8 minutes, stirring well.

Melt the remaining butter with the soft brown sugar and brush the sheets of pastry with the mixture.

Preheat the oven to 170°C (fan oven 150°C), Gas Mark 3½.

Fill the cocottes two-thirds full with the apples and prunes then sprinkle with a little syrup.

Crumple the sheets of pastry in your hands then use to top the cocottes.

Cook for 6–7 minutes, keeping an eye on them to make sure they don't get too brown. Serve immediately.

Pumpkin, chestnut and vanilla cream

Preparation time: 25 minutes +
  cooling
Cooking time: 25 minutes
Serves 4–6

800 g (1 lb 12 oz) pumpkin,
  peeled and sliced
225 g (8 oz) caster sugar
7 pinches of vanilla powder
3 eggs
350 ml (12 fl oz) single cream
200 ml (7 fl oz) milk
20 chestnuts

Place the pumpkin in a large
saucepan with 125 g (4½ oz) of the
sugar, 3 pinches of vanilla powder and
500 ml (18 fl oz) of water. Cook over a
medium heat until the liquid has
evaporated.

Meanwhile, beat the eggs and the
rest of the sugar together vigorously
then add the cream, milk and
remaining vanilla powder and beat
again.

Half fill a roasting tin with hot water
and place the cocottes in it.

Preheat the oven to 150°C (fan oven
130°C), Gas Mark 2.

Cut the pumpkin into large cubes and
share between the cocottes. Sprinkle
with the chestnuts then add the
vanilla cream.

Cook for around 25 minutes. Remove
the cocottes from the roasting tin and
leave to cool at room temperature.
Keep in the fridge and serve cold.

Index

Conversion tables

The tables below are only approximate and are meant to be used as a guide only.

Approximate American/ European conversions

	USA	Metric	Imperial
brown sugar	1 cup	170 g	6 oz
butter	1 stick	115 g	4 oz
butter/ margarine/ lard	1 cup	225 g	8 oz
caster and granulated sugar	2 level tablespoons	30 g	1 oz
caster and granulated sugar	1 cup	225 g	8 oz
currants	1 cup	140 g	5 oz
flour	1 cup	140 g	5 oz
golden syrup	1 cup	350 g	12 oz
ground almonds	1 cup	115 g	4 oz
sultanas/ raisins	1 cup	200 g	7 oz

Approximate American/ European conversions

American	European
1 teaspoon	1 teaspoon/ 5 ml
½ fl oz	1 tablespoon/ ½ fl oz/ 15 ml
¼ cup	4 tablespoons/ 2 fl oz/ 50 ml
½ cup plus 2 tablespoons	¼ pint/ 5 fl oz/ 150 ml
1¼ cups	½ pint/ 10 fl oz/ 300 ml
1 pint/ 16 fl oz	1 pint/ 20 fl oz/ 600 ml
2½ pints (5 cups)	1.2 litres/ 2 pints
10 pints	4,5 litres/ 8 pints

Liquid measures

Imperial	ml	fl oz
1 teaspoon	5	
2 tablespoons	30	
4 tablespoons	60	
¼ pint/ 1 gill	150	5
⅓ pint	200	7
½ pint	300	10
¾ pint	425	15
1 pint	600	20
1¾ pints	1000 (1 litre)	35

Oven temperatures

American	Celsius	Fahrenheit	Gas Mark
Cool	130	250	½
Very slow	140	275	1
Slow	150	300	2
Moderate	160	320	3
Moderate	180	350	4
Moderately hot	190	375	5
Fairly hot	200	400	6
Hot	220	425	7
Very hot	230	450	8
Extremely hot	240	475	9

Other useful measurements

Measurement	Metric	Imperial
1 American cup	225 ml	8 fl oz
1 egg, size 3	50 ml	2 fl oz
1 egg white	30 ml	1 fl oz
1 rounded tablespoon flour	30 g	1 oz
1 rounded tablespoon cornflour	30 g	1 oz
1 rounded tablespoon caster sugar	30 g	1 oz
2 level teaspoons gelatine	10 g	¼ oz